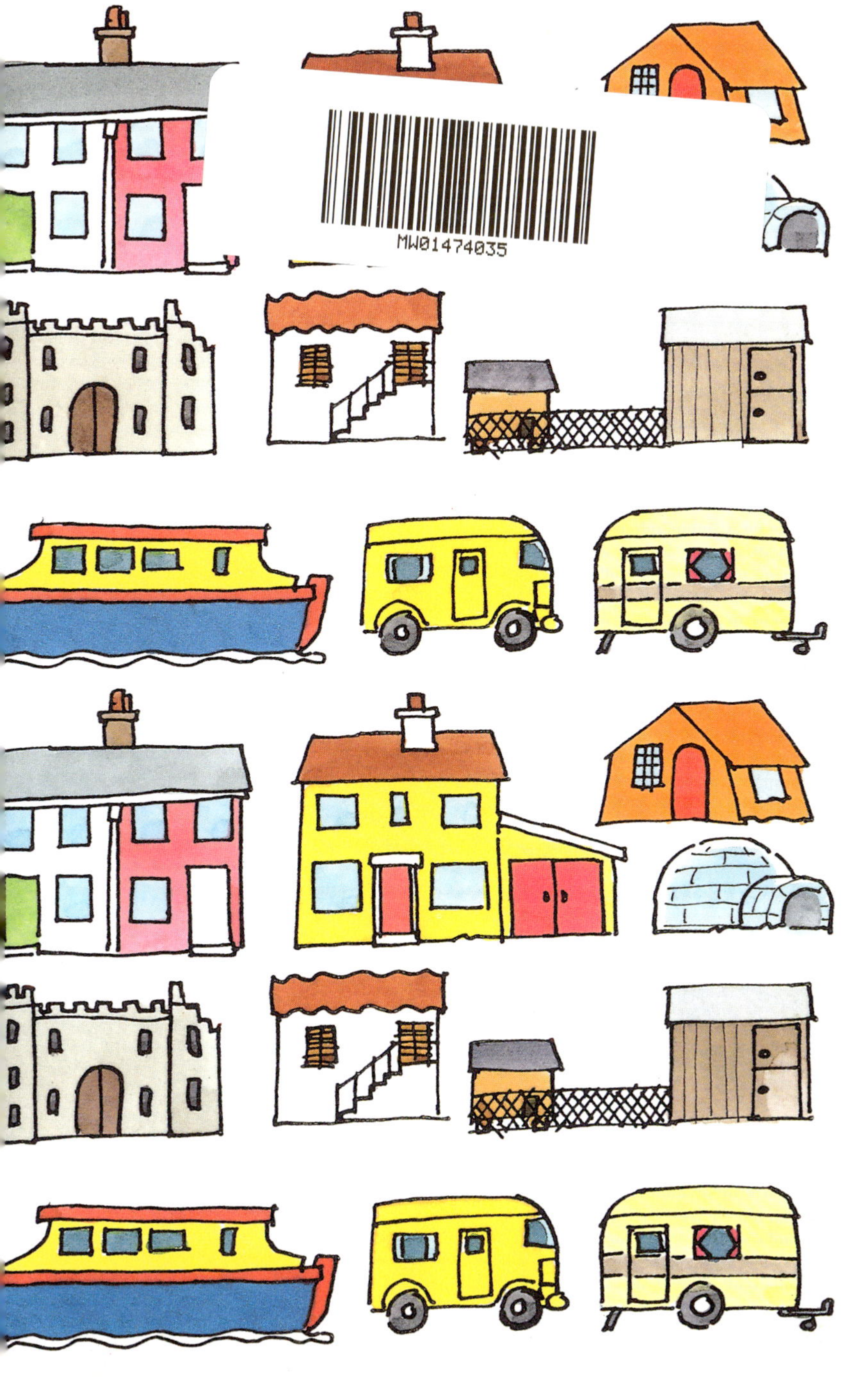

ABOUT THIS BOOK

The first and most important place in a child's life is his or her own home, but more important still are the people in that home and the life they lead together as a family. A home is not just a collection of rooms but a place which is full of life and meaning for all of us.

We have started this book in the child's own home and explored some of the happy events which take place there. As you enjoy these familiar scenes together try to point out things which have happened in your home to encourage your child to think about his or her life in the family.

We hope to broaden the child's understanding by showing many different kinds of homes, from those found in different parts of the world to the homes which animals build.

Enjoy reading together, discuss what is happening in each picture and encourage your child to spot even the smallest details. You will not only pave the way to independent reading, but you will also be developing in your child that vital love of books.

James Fitzsimmons
(Cert. Ed., Head of Infants)

Rhona Whiteford
(B.A. (Open), Cert. Ed., former Head of Infants)

my home

written by
James Fitzsimmons and
Rhona Whiteford

illustrated by Terry Burton

Filmset in Nelson Teaching Alphabet
by kind permission of
Thomas Nelson and Son Ltd.

Copyright © 1990 by World International Publishing Limited.
All rights reserved.
Published in Great Britain by World International Publishing Limited,
An Egmont Company, Egmont House, P.O. Box 111, Great Ducie Street,
Manchester M60 3BL.
Printed in DDR.
ISBN 0 7235 4477 8

A CIP catalogue record for this book is available from the British Library.

my home

My home is where I live with my family.
We have lots of happy times there
with relatives, friends and neighbours.

Have you had a party like this at your home?

the kitchen

At meal times we gather round the table.

There are good things to eat and we always have much to talk about.
What is your favourite thing to eat?

my bedroom

I sometimes invite my friends home and we play in my bedroom.

What kind of bed do you sleep in?

the bathroom

I love bathtime, especially when everything gets wet and I make mountains of bubbles in the water.

Do you have a favourite bathtime toy?

the country

Some people live in houses in the country where there are trees and open fields all around.

Do you see horses or tractors near your home?

the town

Towns can be busy and crowded places to live as people rush to work or to the shops.

Do you have a busy road outside your house?

castles

A very long time ago, some people lived in huge buildings called castles.

Have you ever been to visit a castle?

a cold land

In some snowy lands, homes can be made from blocks of snow and ice. They are very warm and cosy inside.

Would you like to live in a house like this?

a warm land

In warm countries, there are shutters on the windows so that the houses can be kept cool on hot days.

How do you keep cool on a hot day?

pets' homes

Our pets need the right kind of home to keep them happy and healthy.

Can you see a pet you would like?

wild animals' homes

Wild animals make their own safe homes above the ground, under the ground and in the trees.

mobile homes

A mobile home can travel
from place to place.
Have you been in one?

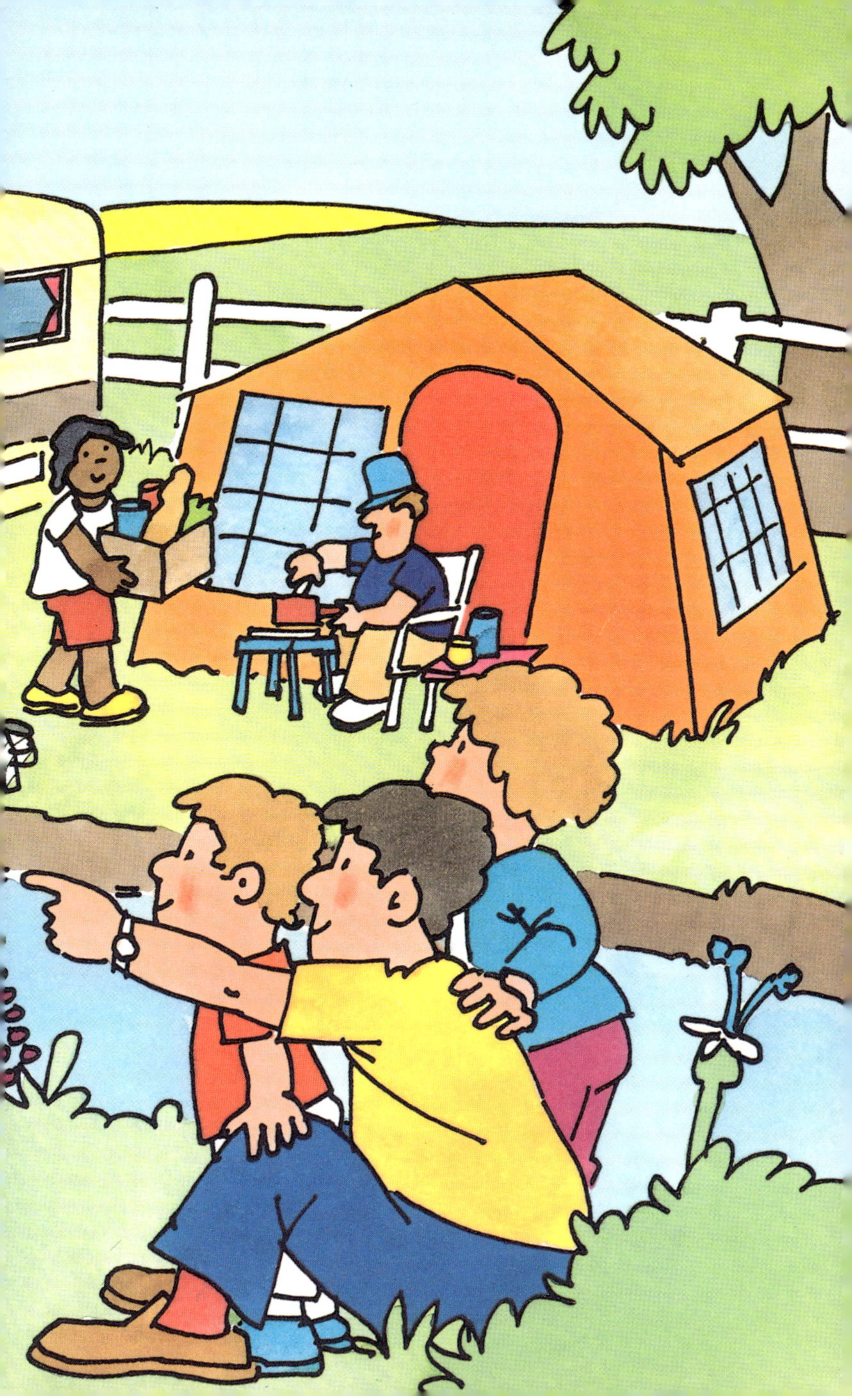

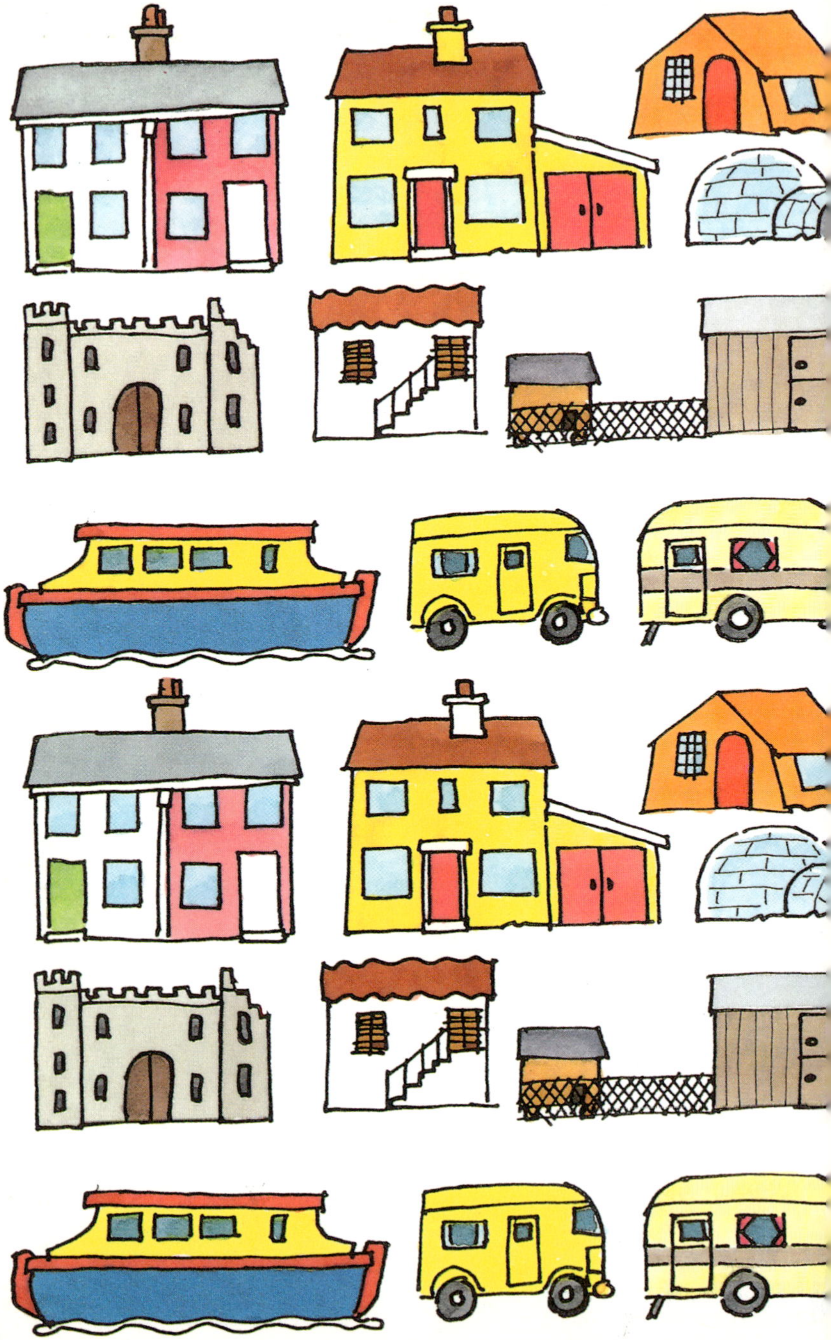